Native Americans of the Southwest

A Journey of Discovery

Tito Naranjo

RUNNING PRESS · PHILADELPHIA, PENNSYLVANIA

Canadian representatives: General Publishing Co., Ltd., 30 Lesmill Road, Don Mills, Ontario M3B 2T6.

International representatives: Worldwide Media Services, Inc., 30 Montgomery Street, Jersey City, New Jersey 07302.

9 8 7 6 5 4 3 2 1
Digit on the right indicates the number of this printing.

Library of Congress Cataloging-in-Publication Number 92–50802

ISBN 1–56138–241–8

Package and cover design by Toby Schmidt
Book interior design, hand lettering, and illustrations by Christian Benton
Additional interior illustrations by Nancy Burpee Schwamm
Picture research by Elizabeth Broadrup
Edited by David Borgenicht

Package back photographs: © Stephen Trimble (top), © Jerry Sieve/Adstock (bottom).
Package illustration: Bob Walters.
Package interior background: © Stephen Trimble.

Book cover: © Jeff Kida/Adstock.

Book interior photographs: © Marcia Keegan: pp. 8, 28, 41, 44 (detail), 45, 51, 52, 53, 57, 60. © Mark Knohl, courtesy New Mexico Magazine: p. 7. Courtesy Museum of New Mexico: p. 15 (Edward S. Curtis, Neg. 89929), p. 17 (detail) (Neg. 80821), p. 29 (Edward S. Curtis, Neg. 144523), p. 30 (detail) (Carl N. Werntz, Neg. 37526), p. 33 (William H. Simpson, Neg. 37696), p. 34 (Ben Wittick, Neg. 58849), p. 35 (H. F. Robinson, Neg. 21618), p. 37 (detail) (Edward S. Curtis, Neg. 144547), p. 38 (Jesse L. Nusbaum, Neg. 28689), p. 40 (detail) (Edward S. Curtis, Neg. 143743). Courtesy National Park Service/Mesa Verde National Park: p. 12. © Stephen Trimble: pp. 14, 16 (detail), 18, 47, 48 (detail), 54, 61.

The poem on page 61 by Nora Naranjo-Morse from *Mud Woman: Poems from the Clay*, Sun Tracks, Volume 20, copyright © 1992 by Nora Naranjo-Morse, is reprinted by permission of the University of Arizona Press.

Typography ITC Garamond by Deborah Lugar

This package may be ordered by mail from the publisher.
Please add $2.50 for postage and handling.
But try your bookstore first!
Running Press Book Publishers
125 South Twenty-second Street
Philadelphia, Pennsylvania 19103–4399

CONTENTS

PART

ONE

The Tewa Emergence Legend

Before there was life on top of the earth, the Tewa (TAY-wah) Pueblo Indians lived underneath a lake. Spirit beings and animals lived nearby.

Two spirit beings, Corn Mother Close-to-Summer and Corn Mother Close-to-Winter, asked the people who would be willing to lead everyone to the earth's surface above. Three times the Corn Mothers asked, and three times they found no volunteers.

The fourth time, one man agreed to go. The Corn Mothers said to him, "You will be a man *and* a woman for all the people." He understood. He became the Hunt Chief—the one who would lead the Tewa people up from beneath the lake to live on the Above.

The Hunt Chief began his journey to the surface. First he went to a higher level of the lake, where all the animals lived. The animals were frightened to see a man, so they scratched him all over. The Hunt Chief became frightened too, and when the animals saw this, they realized that he meant them no harm. The animals mended his wounds and gave him a bow and arrow, an eagle feather for his hair, and black mud to paint his face.

"Now you are ready," the animals told him, "We love you." Hunt Chief returned to his people and began to dance and to sing and call out, "Hu, hu, hu, hai . . ."

The two Corn Mothers said, "You have done well, so far. But you need leaders on the Above."

Again, Corn Mother Close-to-Summer and Corn Mother Close-to-Winter walked among the people. They stopped before another man and gave him a beautiful ear of blue corn.

They told him, "You will be Summer Leader, a mother and a father to the people. Treat your children well. If any man or woman speaks against you, do not become angry."

The Jemez Mountains of New Mexico—home to the Tewa people

They stopped before a third man and gave him a beautiful ear of white corn. They told him, "You will be Winter Leader, a mother and a father to the people. Treat your children well. If a man or woman speaks against you, do not become angry."

The Corn Mothers made two assistants to the Summer and Winter Leaders—called *T'owa* é (T-oh-wah-AY). They sent the T'owa é up to the surface first.

At that time, the people did not know the six directions. They knew only two—Above and Below. So the T'owa é had to create the four compass directions. They threw a handful of mud in each direction—North, South, East, and West.

7

Where the mud hit, a mountain rose and made a boundary on the surface of the earth—a sacred place for the Tewa to live.

When they were done, Hunt Chief, Summer Leader, and Winter Leader led the people out from the lake.

Winter and Summer Leaders took the places of the spirit Corn Mothers below, and became known as "Little Mothers," even though they were men.

When the Tewa people first emerged from the lake, they could not walk upon the surface—it was too soft. Summer Mother turned to Winter Mother and said, "Younger-older, you try."

Winter Mother stepped upon the earth, and immediately the ground froze.

Today, members of the Hunt Society still perform the traditional dance to ensure a successful hunt.

The people could now begin their journey south. But as they walked, some people became sick, and some became unhappy. The Mothers above could not help them, so they led them back under the lake to ask the spirits for help.

The Corn Mothers gave them the Medicine Society and medicine men to help cure their diseases, and the Clown Society, Kossa (Kohs-SA), to make them laugh and to cure sadness and sorrow.

Two more times Winter and Summer Leaders took the people back to the lake. They needed a Hunt Society to find food, a War Society to defend themselves, and they needed a Woman's Society to give women power to heal, cure, and perform ceremonies.

As they continued their journey on the surface, the people came to the Rio Grande River. The Summer Mother turned toward the western mountains, and his people followed. The Winter Mother turned toward the eastern mountains, and his people followed.

After many years, the people came together again and built pueblos in the Southwest.

And they have been there ever since.

PART

TWO

THE PUEBLO PEOPLE

The Pueblo Indians of the Southwest United States are a unique people.

Their ancestors have lived in the Southwest for more than 10,000 years. The Pueblos built five-story buildings long before the Spanish, English, and other explorers came to the United States. And they have kept their beliefs and way of life throughout 450 years of contact with other cultures. In this book, you will learn about that way of life.

Many Native American peoples live in the Southwest, with many different cultures—including the Pueblo people, the Navajos, and the Apaches. Today, the Pueblo people are the Western and Eastern Keresan, the Zuni, some of the Hopi people, and the Tanoan people. In this book you will meet Pueblos, witness Tewa dances and ceremonies, and share a typical day on the Pueblo—both past and present. And you can piece

The first pueblos were cliff dwellings—such as Mesa Verde in Colorado, built by the Anasazi people in the 13th century.

together and decorate an authentic clay bowl—a reminder of the Southwest heritage.

The Tewa Emergence Legend tells us something of traditional Pueblo beliefs—but to learn Pueblo history, we must look elsewhere. The word "Pueblo" was first used by Spanish priests and explorers who came to the Southwest in 1540. They used the term to refer to the permanent villages they found—villages built entirely of rock, or of sun-dried bricks made of mud mixed with straw, called *adobe* (uh-DOH-bee).

Today, the Pueblo Indians live in North Central Arizona and in Western and North Central New Mexico in 28 different pueblos.

All Pueblo people speak one of four different languages—Tanoan, Keresan, Zunian, and Shoshonean. Each language has several variations called *dialects*. Even though these dialects are related, people who speak different dialects cannot understand each other.

Most Tewa people live in New Mexico, and today, there are between 5,000 and 6,000 Tewa Pueblo Indians. The Tewa belong to the Tanoan (tuh-NO-un) language group, and speak either Tewa, Tiwa, or Towa. (The Tewa people call themselves Towa.) It is this group that we will visit—and discover their lifestyle, culture, and beliefs.

SEEKING LIFE

The guiding principle of the Tewa people is "Seeking Life." To "seek life" means to truly *be* Tewa, as their ancestors were and their children will be. It is to follow the Tewa ways; to live in the present with a spiritual connection to the past. In seeking life, the Tewa people look to the future beyond life as a return to the lake, where all life began.

As in the legend, the Tewa people are led by Winter and Summer Mothers, who help the Tewa Indians seek life through dances, ceremonies, and beliefs. The Mothers are religious leaders, called *caciques*. They also decide who will fill positions in the Pueblo government.

Everyone who lives in a Tewa Pueblo belongs to either the Winter or Summer people. Tewa children become members of the Summer or Winter people at birth, depending on their parent's group. The group to which a person belongs determines their involvement in ceremonial life. But these divisions are not permanent, and individuals may change membership through marriage or by choice.

Each group performs dances or other ceremonies during the time of year when its cacique leads the Pueblo. The Summer Mother leads from March to October, and the Summer people

Two children, seeking life, perform the corn dance in Santa Clara Pueblo, New Mexico.

Harvest time at San Juan Pueblo, 1905

perform the Corn Dance and other summer dances. The Winter Mother leads from October to March, and the Winter people perform the Deer Dance and other winter dances. The split in the Pueblo between the Summer people and the Winter people does not separate the Tewa. They come together through membership in other societies, such as the Hunt Society, the Medicine Society, the Women's Society, the Clown Society, and the Scalp or War Society. These societies preserve beliefs and perform ceremonies, dances, and rituals for the good of the Pueblo. When an individual joins one of these groups, he or she becomes both a Summer *and* a Winter person—a "made" or "finished" person who is said to belong to the middle, or both sides.

All Pueblo Indians observe a religious calendar based on the movement of the sun. This calendar determines when important events will happen—harvest dances, hunt dances, relay races to nourish the sun, quiet time for the earth to rest, drama of the Cloud Spirits, and planting time.

By this calendar, from birth to death, the Tewa people seek life. To them, death is a transition from living on the earth to becoming a spirit again, and returning to below the Lake where all Tewa life once began.

THE FIRST PUEBLO PEOPLE

The story of the first Pueblos can be told in several ways—through ancient legend and through modern science. Archaeologists think that ancestors of the Pueblos crossed the land bridge over the Bering Straits between Alaska and Russia about 10,000 years ago.

Recent scientific evidence leads archaeologists to think that ancestors of the Pueblo people may have lived and hunted in the Southwest as long as 40,000 years ago. Arrowheads and other stone tools found together with mastodon bones in New Mexico help prove this.

From 300 to 100 B.C., three distinct Southwestern cultures began to appear— the Anasazi, the Mogollon, and the Hohokam. Archae- ologists think that the Anasazi and the Mogollon peoples were the forerun- ners of the present day Pueblo cultures, because of where they lived, and artifacts they left behind.

From around A.D. zero to around A.D. 500, people

Rock art, like this Anasazi petro- glyph, provides evidence of ancient pueblo life in the cliffs.

learned how to plant crops. This knowledge came from Indians in Mexico, where farming was already advanced.

During this time, people also began to shift from a wandering life to a settled life. People formed small villages in caves and rock shelters in the Four Corners area (where the borders of Arizona, New Mexico, Colorado, and Utah meet). Animals began to be raised for food. Baskets appeared, and pottery-making began. Life was becoming easier.

As home became more permanent, villages grew and became more advanced. Some buildings had as many as 100 rooms, and circular underground religious rooms called *kivas* appeared, with built-in benches, central firepits, ventilator shafts for air, and a *sipapu* (a symbolic hole of entry to the underworld).

Later periods brought better strains of corn, primitive irrigation, and new and varied forms of pottery. In the years from 1100 to 1300, as Anasazi culture began to spread, great

pueblos were built all over the Southwest. This was classic Pueblo architecture: well-planned, multi-storied dwellings around central plazas.

As the Pueblo centers such as Chaco Canyon in New Mexico, Mesa Verde in Colorado, and the Kayenta and Hopi Mesas in Arizona grew, more food and shelter were needed. People began to move south.

The Great Kiva at Chaco Canyon, New Mexico, was a major center of early pueblo religious life.

From 1300 to 1600, the

Adobe bricks drying beside a Catholic church at Picuris Pueblo—symbolic of Pueblo culture past and present.

Anasazi left the high mesa country of the Four Corners area. They built large pueblos with up to 1,000 rooms along the Rio Grande, on mesas, and around the Zuni and Acoma pueblos.

But in the years from 1546 to 1696, the Spanish conquistadors came north from Mexico, bringing warfare and disease, and many pueblos were abandoned.

More changes came later—radio and TV, airplanes, social changes that led to intermarriage, and the change from sharing and trading to an economy based on money. But despite outside influences, the Pueblo people struggle to protect and preserve their culture.

PART

THREE

Excavate and Reconstruct
Your Own Bowl

Now you can help to preserve one of the artifacts of the Pueblo people. Your own example of Anasazi pottery from the Basketmaker II period (1100–1300) lies within the slab of rock contained in this kit. So get ready to excavate!

Get Ready
In this kit you'll find:
- a rectangular slab of rock (this holds the pieces of your replica Anasazi bowl)
- a wooden spatula to dig out the pieces of pottery
- a paint disc and paintbrush

You'll also need:
- newspaper or a plastic bag to cover your work surface
- water
- a bucket or basin in which to soak the slab of rock
- a soft brush (a paintbrush or old toothbrush)
- paper towels
- white glue (such as Elmer's Glue-All)

Excavate Your Artifact
An archaeological expedition rarely finds an undamaged artifact—pottery is usually found in many pieces and has to be restored and reassembled. That's your job.

The pottery in this kit is embedded in a mixture of clay and pumice—a light clay similar to that found in New Mexico. The bowl is an authentic replica of a vessel excavated by Earl Morris in 1926 in Mimbres, New Mexico. The bowl was found in a grave site, with its bottom knocked out—possibly to free the spirit of the pot so that it could accompany the person with whom it was buried.

Your first step is to excavate the pieces of pottery from

the clay. Take your time and do it carefully—allow at least an hour. This can be messy, too, so work outdoors or indoors on a covered, easy-to-clean surface. Cover your work area with a newspaper or plastic bag.

1) Fill the bucket or basin with water halfway. Place the slab of rock in the water. Let it soak at least five minutes. Remove the slab and pat it dry. (Don't pour out the water just yet.)

2) Using the spatula (or some other tool, such as a plastic knife, an old toothbrush, or toothpicks), dig out the pieces of pottery. Carefully scrape away the soft clay. If the clay doesn't scrape away easily, soak the block some more.

Be careful while you're handling the pottery— some of the pieces may be sharp! Work slowly and try not to damage any pottery. If you do, don't worry— you can glue them together later.

3) Clean the pottery pieces by rinsing them in the bucket and brushing them with your soft brush. Be sure to clean the edges well—they must be dirt-free to bond well with the glue. When all the pieces are clean, pour the leftover clay and water into the ground outside or

23

into a disposable container, not down the drain.

Pat the pottery pieces with a paper towel, and let them sit out overnight on a sheet of newspaper. (To speed up the drying process, you can use a hair dryer.)

Remember, reconstructing an artifact is a precise, painstaking process. Be patient.

4) After the pieces are dry, find the ones that fit together. Think of it as a jigsaw puzzle and take it one piece at a time.

5) Now you're ready to reconstruct. Using the glue, join two pieces at a time, edge to edge. Apply the glue and hold the pieces together at least 30 seconds. Don't worry about excess glue—you can scrape it away after it's dry. Press the pieces together firmly, but not too hard. Then, carefully set the glued pieces out to dry. Wait as long as the glue bottle tells you to wait—usually about 30 minutes to an hour.

Once your first set of pieces is dry, glue them together. Soon, with care and patience, you will have reconstructed your artifact!

6) Now you can decorate the bowl. An outline of the authentic Anasazi design that once covered the bowl is already printed on it.

First, trace the design with a pencil. It will be easier to see while you paint.

The paint disc in the kit works like the paint in a set of watercolors. Dip the brush in water and dab it on the paint disc until some of the paint smears on the brush. Now, paint the design, using a small amount of paint so that you don't smudge. Don't worry if you make a mistake on the design— just scrape the paint off and repaint it later.

When you're done, let it dry all day or overnight.

This bowl, like the one the Anasazi used more than 500 years ago, will help you remember Pueblo cultures of the past!

Let's see what those cultures were, and still are, like.

The final result—an authentic replica of an Anasazi bowl

PART

FOUR

Puye Pueblo, 1350 A.D.

At Puye Pueblo, some of the early multi-storied dwellings still stand today.

A top *a volcanic rock mesa—a high, flat mountain in New Mexico—stands a large Tewa pueblo that was occupied around 1300 A.D. Its name is Puye (pooh-YAY), meaning "where rabbits meet."*

Originally, the Tewa people dug caves in the soft rock cliffs. But as they learned how to build with stone blocks, they made multi-storied houses on the face of the cliff to cover the caves.

The people of Puye were farmers, hunters, and gatherers. They planted beans, corn, and squash in the fields behind the Pueblo and depended on rain for crop growth. They also hunted deer, elk, mountain sheep, and small game in the Jemez Mountains behind the Pueblo.

Between 300 and 400 persons once lived at Puye. Here is a day in their life.

June 21, 1350—Dawn sent rays of light over the high eastern mountains as smoke from cooking fires curled from rooftops. Old men draped in tanned elkskin blankets walked east to say prayers and offer blue cornmeal to the spirits before sunrise.

Prayer was important today. Sun Father was to make his longest journey of the year in the sky over Puye—it was the longest day of the year. The Summer Leader had been keeping track of Sun Father's journey on a high wall at his retreat.

A quiet boy lived at Puye with his parents and two

Life at Santa Clara Pueblo in the early 1900s

29

sisters. His name was Sokuwa P'iin (Soh-koo-WAH p-EEN), or Foggy Mountain. Sokuwa had seen nine summers. His father and mother were Nana Tsa (NAH-nah TSAH), or White Aspen, and Khuun Tsan (KOO-oon TSAHN), Early Corn.

Sokuwa's older sister, Ojegi (oh-jay-GHEE), or Evergreen Mist, was twelve. His favorite sister, however, was Plains Flower, or Povi (poh-VEE). At harvest time, Povi would turn

To the Pueblo people, weaving is an important tradition passed on from generation to generation.

nine. She wore her black hair in braids and was curious about everything.

Povi loved to count. There was so much to see and do at the Pueblo that counting helped her keep track. This day she was counting the strings on her father's weaving loom as everyone prepared for the day's activities.

ACTIVITY: Counting in Tewa

Learn to count from one to ten in Tewa! Here are the numbers and their pronunciations:

one	we (weh)
two	weje (WEH-jay)
three	poje (POH-jay)
four	jonu (JOE-new)
five	p'anu (p-AH-new)
six	sí (see)
seven	t'sé (t-SEH)
eight	khave (KAH-vay)
nine	kwhenu (KWAY-new)
ten	t'e aa (t-AY-ah-ah)

First, read the list out loud several times. Then, with a sheet of paper, cover the Tewa side of the list. Now try to remember each Tewa number. Only look if you have to! Practice until you can remember all ten words.

Now that you know all ten words, find objects in your room to count like Povi. Think of other counting games and songs. Play and sing them in Tewa instead of English. Then teach a friend how to count in Tewa.

Sokuwa heard his father walk out early from their home. His mother was dressing and brushing her hair with a stiff, bundled grass stalk.

At Puye, Pueblo children learned respectful behavior toward adults early, so everyone older was called either aunt or uncle. Close relatives who had children were called *tara* (TAH-dah), the Tewa word for father, or *jia* (GEE-ah), the Tewa word for mother.

Sokuwa's mother, who the children called Jia, said to her children, "The men will be running soon. Dress quickly, girls—wear your woven blankets today. Today we give our strength and breath to Father Sun and run the Sun Race." When they were all ready, they went outside.

As they stood along the race course, the sound of men singing the chant of the Sun Races came down the path. Two lines of Summer people and two lines of Winter people sang, standing across from each other on the course. After the chant, the lines separated. One line of each group went to the west end of the course, and the other went to the east.

Sokuwa would run in the relay races next year. He would be initiated in the coming spring to recognize that he was of the Winter People, a Winter Man. Then he, too, could run in the foot races to give nourishment to Father Sun.

Women began to trill high-pitched sounds of, "Li, li, li, li . . . " With that, two young runners ran east in their bare feet, each one wearing an eagle feather in his hair that flowed

On pueblos, racers do not run to compete, but to participate in ceremonies to give thanks.

behind as he sped along the course.

When the first two runners reached the east end, two runners ran back to the west end. Back and forth, they continued—the Summer men were clearly ahead. But the race was not for competition. Winter Mother and Summer Mother stood before the four lines of runners after the race and they said the traditional prayer:

> *Children of the spirits*
> *Children of Winter and Summer*
> *Today we have given of our breath*
> *Today we have given strength of our legs*
> *Children of Sun Father*
> *Children of the Lake*
> *Today we have been seeking life*
> *Today we have given life to Sun Father*
> *Today we have received life in return.*

Sokuwa and Povi watched the runners with their grand-father. After the race, Sokuwa and Povi ran too—along the tops of the cliffs outside the Pueblo walls, and then back home.

Home was two rooms in the Pueblo. Each room was about the size of a small modern bedroom. Inside, the bricks were plastered with mud to keep out cold and rain. Across from the small doorway stood a large fireplace used for heating and cooking. A weaving loom sat opposite the fireplace, under-neath a small round window. On it, Nana made blankets and clothing, and Jia made women's woven cotton dresses called *mantas* (MAHN-tahz). (These traditional Pueblo garments are decorated at the bottom in red, green, or black. They are worn diagonally across the body to leave the left shoulder bare.)

Today, Sokuwa's father had gone into the Winter Kiva (a religious room) to pray and to dance the Corn Grinding Dance.

The inside of a Zuni house—an example of early 20th-century Pueblo architecture

So Sokuwa asked his grandfather if Povi could come to the corn fields with them to work, since his father would not be going.

Grandfather said, "Yes—and she can help dig and carry clay on the way home." It was an honor for children to help with the work.

After a morning meal, Sokuwa and Povi walked with their grandfather to the corn and bean fields west of Puye. A mile away from Puye mesa, the three passed through "Little Warm Canyon," a dry canyon called an *arroyo*. The arroyo filled with water after heavy rainstorms, or when mountain snows melted in the spring.

As he walked, Grandfather used his digging stick as a cane—later he would use it to dig for clay. When they reached the corn fields, Grandfather asked the children to walk the

A Hopi man uses his digging stick.

edges of the fields to chase off jack rabbits, wild turkeys, or other animals that might try to eat the corn.

Sokuwa carried a foot-long throwing stick made from an oak root. He practiced throwing this "rabbit stick" at various targets as he and Povi walked. Povi carried a worn leather pouch that held stones for her to throw.

Across an arroyo and through a glade of pinon trees, Sokuwa and Povi heard boys calling to each other as their fathers worked. There in the large fields, a summer pueblo was being built. The pueblo there was to be used only in the summer, when the ripening corn needed constant protection from animals.

Sokuwa and Povi knew that a good corn harvest would give them food all winter. Corn was used to make a blue corn meal drink called *atole* (ah-TOLL-ay), a blue corn bread (like a modern doughnut hole) called *sakewe* (sah-keh-WEH), and a thin paper bread called *buwa* (boo-WAH).

While the children walked, Grandfather loosened dirt from the bases of the corn plants with his digging stick. Using his hands, he scooped dirt toward the bases of the stalks and pressed the dirt into a solid mound. He did this to help the corn stalks grow higher roots to support the plants as they grew taller.

When the children arrived from their walk along the edges of the fields, he asked, "My children, what did you see?"

Sokuwa said, "All we saw were deer tracks going down to the water holes." The plants were safe from animals.

The three worked together, pulling weeds and piling dirt around the young plants until the sun began to go down. On the way back to the pueblo, they detoured into Little Warm Canyon. They went to the embankments and dug out large chunks of clay with bright mica flecks. This clay would be used to make cooking pots.

A Tewa woman fills her water jar from the Rio Grande river near San Ildefonso Pueblo in 1905. Different types of pottery were used to store food and water, and for decoration.

Grandfather brought along a pack made from elk hide to carry the heavy clay. The pack had a strap which could be placed on the forehead, to support its weight. Sokuwa and Povi also had parts of old elk hides to carry smaller amounts of clay. They tied the ends of their hides to three-foot sticks, to balance the load on their shoulders.

The trio walked slowly onto Puye mesa as the sun sent long shadows over the landscape. In the middle of the pueblo, the Corn Grinding Dance had begun.

Sixteen men danced in a line. Their hair was unbraided, and they wore large necklaces of evergreen boughs. Their upper bodies were painted dark gray, with a large white V on each man's chest. They wore cotton woven skirts, and turtle shells tied around their right knees clacked with each dance step as they sang the song of the Corn Grinding Dance.

A woman grinds corn at Zuni Pueblo, c. 1910. Corn was a major food source to the pueblos, and could be ground into flour for many different uses.

In front of the dancers sat two women, grinding corn on a bowl-shaped stone called a *metate* (meh-TAH-tay). An older man knelt at the head of the row of dancers, beating a steady rhythm on a rolled elk hide with a stick.

Earlier in the day, between dances, Sokuwa and Povi's mother Jia (GEE-ah) and sister Ojegi, sat on the roof of their house to make a large pot. Jia used the bottom third of a large gourd called a *puki* (pooh-KEE) to start it. Ojegi made coils from the clay while Jia joined them to the inside of the pot and smoothed them. In the end, the pot was about a foot high and wide.

After the pot was set down to dry inside the house, Jia and Ojegi tended a stew of deer meat mixed with dried corn in another pot. It sat covered with hot coals for most of the day. When the sun reached its highest point in the sky, Jia and Ojegi carried stew down into the kiva for the men who were dancing.

After the Corn Grinding Dance, the family ate. Puye people ate two meals a day—one in the morning and one at the end of the day. The family gathered in a circle around the pot of stew. Each one had a gourd ladle to dip out stew, and they ate right from the ladle. Along with the stew, Jia had made a small basketful of buwa.

After the evening meal, Sokuwa and Povi asked Tapovi to help them make a toy—a gourd buzzer called a *pothini* (poh-THEE-nee). They cut two circular disks from a gourd and poked two holes in the center of each disk. Then they threaded buckskin strips through the holes and held the strips in opposite hands. By pulling their hands apart and bringing them back together, the disks gave off a roaring sound.

Then they went outside to play a game like marbles—*naanbewe* (nah-ahn-beh-WAY). In this game, children placed

marble-shaped, hard clay pieces in mounds of dirt. From a distance, they threw a flat rock towards the mounds. The object was to be the first to uncover all the round clay marbles.

Grandfather also enjoyed playing this game, but tonight he would not play. He was tired from the day's work, so he slept in his adjoining room. In Jia's family the women slept in the front room and men slept in the back. They all slept on mats of elk or buffalo hide and used soft buckskin or woven rabbit fur blankets for covers.

A Tewa girl from Nambe Pueblo, 1905

But before falling asleep, Povi and Ojegi played another game. Povi tickled Ojegi and messed up her hair. Then, in Tewa, they chanted,

"Wrinkles, Wrinkles, may you go to sleep young, but may you wake up wrinkled like an old lady." And they laughed themselves to sleep.

It was a good day.

ACTIVITY: Have a Tewa Breakfast

Atole was, and still is, a favorite morning food for the Tewa people. This corn meal gruel is easy to make, and good for you, too! Here's how.

Atole—breakfast of the Tewa

What you need:
> 3 ½ cups of water
> 2 heaping tablespoons of blue or yellow cornmeal
> Milk, honey, or sugar to taste

What to do:
In a bowl, mix the cornmeal with ½ cup of cold water. Boil 3 cups of water in a medium saucepan.

Add the cornmeal mixture to the boiling water. Stir until the mixture becomes thick, but is still pourable.

Pour into a cup, and add milk, honey, or sugar to your taste. Let it cool slightly before you try it, then drink up and enjoy!

PART

FIVE

Santa Clara Pueblo, 1993

The people who live in Santa Clara Pueblo today descended from the people who lived long ago at Puye. No living person knows why, when, or how they made the move down into the valley below.

Santa Clara is called "the Singing Water Village," because a creek runs nearby. Because this area has a longer growing season than land around Puye, a better source of water, and more planting locations, the people in Santa Clara can live much more easily than their ancestors did.

With about 2,500 people, Santa Clara is considered a large Tewa pueblo. It is best known for the many respected potters, sculptors, and writers who live there.

June 21, 1993—Dawn is just a glow of light over the high Sangre De Cristo Mountains to the east.

Very few cars are out this morning on the highway just west of the pueblo. Tribal police have stopped all traffic, and many people covered with shawls and blankets wait along the dirt road which enters the Pueblo. Inside the Pueblo, around the plaza, many people watch and wait, including an old woman and her two grandchildren.

The woman is nearly 80 years old, and because she is an elder, she is known as

Tewa children today walk a fine line between modern and traditional life.

44

Tewa potters are renowned for their unique style of pottery.

Jia, or Mother. She is a well-known potter who makes *micaceous* (mih-KAY-shus) pottery that contains flecks of mica and silica—the same clay that has always been used by the Tewa potters. Jia's daughters are also well known for making the beautiful red-and-black polished pottery.

The children are her great grandchildren, who stay with her often. Jeng (j-EN), or Otter, is twelve. Kapovi (kah-poh-VEE), or Leaf Flower, is ten and called Povi, for short.

As dawn comes over the eastern mountains, the three of them hear a rifle shot break the stillness of the early summer morning. A drum beat follows the rifle shot, which is followed by men's voices. They sing the song of the Mountain Sheep Dance:

From every mountain peak around us
From their fog-shrouded, cloud-flowering places
They are chasing the dawn
With their rain-bringing ways
They are chasing the dawn
With their mountain-finding ways
They are chasing the dawn
Up on Tsikumu Mountain
Sheep old lady, Ram old man
They are chasing the dawn.

The song is repeated in verses, naming different mountains. It gives thanks for the mountain sheep that were hunted by Tewa men in the past.

Jeng and Povi look up into the hills. Male dancers wearing wild mountain sheep horns on their heads, faces painted black, descend and cross the highway. Two lines of ram dancers pass through the waiting crowd. They are led by a Pueblo man dressed completely in buckskin, his face painted black. He wears a single eagle feather in his hair, carries a bow and arrows, and holds a handful of Douglas fir.

He calls out, "Hu, hu, hu, hai . . ." as he dances. He is the Hunt Chief, the hero of the Emergence Legend.

Jia and other older men and women say Tewa prayers as the singers and dancers pass them. They sprinkle blue corn meal on the ground where the dancers step. This dance at dawn is done in the Pueblo plaza and will be done four more times throughout the rest of the day.

After the first dance, Jia, Jeng, and Povi return to Jia's house. Jia has to fire pottery, so Jeng and Povi help her take pottery pieces out next to a Pueblo ash mound. They help her start a fire around a metal grate which holds the pottery.

A Tewa potter prepares for a second firing with "cow cakes."

When the wood burns down to hot coals, Jia places large, dry, flat cow manure over all the pottery for the second firing. The "cow cakes," as they are called, provide an intense heat that wood cannot match. Soon, the pots are a glowing cherry red. Firing with cow cakes assures a complete firing and leaves black spots on the pots called "fire clouds." This method was used at Puye many hundreds of years ago.

It will take about two hours for Jia's pottery to cool down, so Jia asks Jeng and Povi to walk to their aunt's house outside the pueblo. Jia tells them to ask their aunt, *Ko o* (which means aunt), if she wants to drive up to Puye with them to check on the corn, squash, and melon plants and pull weeds. They like this idea, for Ko o also makes beautiful pottery.

Jeng and Povi's father left early for work at the Los Alamos National Laboratories. When their father speaks about his job, he says strange things that Jeng and Povi don't understand. His job is cell cloning, and he speaks about things like "gene 21"

Taos Pueblo, New Mexico—an example of modern Pueblo architecture

and "Downs syndrome." They are proud of their father—even though they really don't know what his work is. But they understand pottery making well.

Povi would tell her friends, "My dad plays around with some things called the RNAs and DNAs. I don't know what those things are. But my Ko o makes more money selling pottery. Sometimes she sells one of her pieces for as much as my dad makes in lots and lots of days of working. I'm going to make pottery too, after I finish school."

When Jeng and Povi reach Ko o's house, she is using a smooth stone to polish a large Santa Clara pot. The stone has been in the family many hundreds of years.

Ko o says that she has to take one piece of pottery to Santa Fe that afternoon, but she will help the others work the fields as soon as she finishes polishing the pot. When she is done, they walk back to Jia's, get into the car, and head to Puye.

As they drive into the mountains to Puye, 12 miles up the road, Povi and Jeng ask Jia to tell them a story. They love the story of the Turkey Girl who once lived there—so Jia begins.

"A long time ago, when Santa Clara people lived at Puye, there was a girl who lived with her mother and father. They were very poor.

"Turkey Girl took care of the family's turkey flock. They raised the turkeys for food, they used the feathers for ceremonies, and they used the soft down to make blankets.

"Every day, Turkey Girl walked with the flock into the nearby mountains and pine forests. She watched the tame turkeys eat grasses and insects and scratch around for pebbles. But she was lonely. She had no brothers or sisters; she spent most of her days with the turkeys. She even spoke with the big birds—and sometimes believed that they could understand her.

"Her friends made fun of her because she spent too much time with the flock. 'You are even beginning to gobble and cluck like a turkey,' they teased.

"One day, there was a big ceremonial dance and feast at Puye. People were coming from Nava Hu, Shufinne, and other pueblos. But Turkey Girl sat on a hillside crying—she had to tend the flock.

"She wished that she could be dressed in a beautiful manta dress, buckskin moccasins, and shell earrings. She wanted to be in Puye for the day.

"As she sat crying, four of the larger turkeys came up to her and asked why she was sad. She told them that she wanted to be at Puye and to be among the people dressed in beautiful clothes.

"The oldest of the turkeys said, 'We will help you because you take care of us every day. Wait right here and we will go to Puye to get clothes for you.'

"It was not long before the four turkeys were back with a beautiful white woven manta, earrings, a turquoise necklace, beautiful women's moccasins, and a green-and-black sash for Turkey Girl's waist. They took Turkey Girl down to the water along Little Warm Springs Canyon, where they washed and dressed her beautifully.

"The turkeys then led her back to Puye, where she went among the people. No one knew who she was—people thought she must be from the large pueblo to the south. Her friends admired her. Many young men noticed her beauty for the first time that day and wished to marry her when she became older. She had been rewarded for her work."

The car is just below Puye when Jia finishes telling the story. Povi says, "Jia, that story sounds like *Cinderella*. Did Turkey Girl live happily ever after, too? Did she marry a prince?"

Jia says, "The meaning of that story is that the Tewa people work hard. And when we work hard, as in the fields today, even the animals around us will take care of us, and our prayers for Seeking Life will be answered."

ACTIVITY: Become a Storyteller

The Pueblo people have a tradition of telling stories about their history and beliefs. They tell folktales to explain the workings of the world—how it came to be, how it grew, and how to live in it well. You can do the same.

First, gather a group of friends. Sit in a circle.

Next, tell a story that you know. It can be real or not—many Native American legends have some truth to them, as well as elements of fantasy. If you can't think of a story, tell the story of the Turkey Girl to your friends.

Tewa children gather with their elders to hear traditional stories.

Many of the best Native American legends were lessons in culture and belief, so try to tell a story that teaches something.

Then, take turns, and let the stories flow. Make up new stories or add to stories you have been told. You can even make up stories together, taking turns around the circle and each saying a sentence in the story.

Tewa children often help tend the fields, as does this child at San Ildefonso.

At Puye, Ko o, Jia, Jeng, and Povi work for hours—pulling weeds and putting mounds of dirt around corn plants. These are the same plots of land planted more than 600 years ago by Sokuwa and Povi's family.

On the way back, Ko o stops the pickup truck by a small dam. On the other side of the dam is an old footpath. On this path, the ancient people of Puye came down from the mesa to the fields— this was where Grandfather, Sokuwa, and Povi dug for clay long ago.

Today, Povi and Jeng run around the earthen pond looking for dried cow cakes which Jia would use for firing. After half an hour, they all come back with an armload of cakes— which Jia throws into the back of the truck. Off they go again.

Near Santa Clara Pueblo, in the hills to the west, the four stop again to dig clay. Jia says a prayer to Clay Mother:

Even when hunting and fishing, the Tewa people respect the land they live on.

> *Clay Mother*
> *We have come to the place of your abode*
> *We ask your spirit to respect us*
> *May we take of your sacred being today*
> *We pray that you help to feed and clothe us*
> *One day we will become a part of you*
> *Nanchu Kwijo, Kudahwaha.*
> *(Clay mother, thank you.)*

This prayer recognizes that everything in the Tewa people's world is alive—even the dirt, rocks, and clay. Tewa people believe they are connected in spirit to all things—especially the clay. For one day, they too will become clay.

While Jia and Ko o dig, Povi and Jeng play and run on the steep embankment above the clay pit. They slide down it, like

A playful example of modern Tewa sculpture

otters. When the digging and sliding is done, they head back to Santa Clara.

Back in the Pueblo, tourists mill about, waiting in the shade of buildings for the dancers to come out again. The tourists come from Germany, Japan, New York, Los Angeles, Dallas, Philadelphia, Santa Fe, and Albuquerque. For important ceremonial days, Jia and her daughters often feed and welcome visitors.

Sometimes visitors want to pay her for meals. Jia explains to them that Pueblo people believe in sharing and in being generous to everyone without expecting something back.

Povi and Jeng run to watch the third dance of the day— two of their cousins are in this one. When the dancers go into the kiva, Jeng and Povi walk up to Ko o's house under the big cottonwood trees. They call Jia to tell her that they are going to Santa Fe with Ko o.

Jia is busy cooking for the whole family, who will come over to eat when the dance is finished. Everyone looks forward to eating the bread made in the large, beehive-shaped adobe ovens, and the red chili stew—traditional Pueblo fiesta foods. But the dancing is to come first.

The fourth and last dance is being done when Ko o, Jeng, and Povi return to Santa Clara. They walk down to Jia's house in the middle of the Pueblo, where their other aunts and uncles watch. Povi and Jeng's father and mother are there, too—they have come to be with the family.

Of the four Mountain Sheep Dances, the first and the last are the most beautiful. As Jia's family watches, the Hunt Chief leads the dancers into four different areas of the plaza.

The men who dance as mountain sheep lift their right feet in unison to the drumbeats. Men in the chorus tell through motions with evergreen branches how the sacred sheep were

brought to the Pueblo from faraway mountains. Women in black woven mantas, their black hair streaming down, dance with the lightness of air.

At the end, all the dancers, singers, drummers, and men of the chorus motion outward to the people of the audience and say,

"We have been seeking life. We bring you life."

The people say, "May it be so."

And with that, a Pueblo religious ceremony is completed.

After a ceremony is completed, Tewa men return to the kiva to pray.

PART

SIX

TODAY AND TOMORROW ON THE PUEBLO

The most important parts of Pueblo life still take place today in the same way as they did hundreds of years ago at Puye. Pueblo people know that their traditional beliefs are important. Firm commitments to work, to caring for each other, to the family, and to sharing and generosity are made at an early age.

In the pueblos, elders are treated with respect for their knowledge, because Tewa ways are not written in books—they must be taught by word and experience. Young children are also important to the Tewa—they assure the Pueblo that its way of life will continue.

We can all learn something from this way of life. The Pueblo people believe that everything has a soul—rocks, dirt, wind, animals, and plants. They teach respect for everything,

and that we must all strive to protect the world around us. It is, after all, the world in which their fathers lived and their children will dwell.

Many different cultures have tried to change the Pueblo people. Spanish explorers tried to give Pueblo people Catholicism, the Mexican government tried to give the Pueblos a new government, and Americans tried to bring them Protestant religions and constitutional government.

To these visitors, the Pueblos always said, "We

The Tewa people believe in a strong connection between children and adults.

Detail of a Tewa pot

will consider what you want to give us. But we will only add it to our religion and government if our own beliefs can remain intact. We will always be Tewa."

As Nora Naranjo-Morse, a Tewa poet, put it,

> *Yet, somewhere in us*
> *Persistent sounds surge upward*
> *Reminding us of our life cycles,*
> *And the innocent wonder*
> *That is our birthright,*
> *As children of*
> *The Towa.*

May it be so.

ABOUT THE AUTHOR

Tito Naranjo is a Pueblo sculptor, teacher, and writer who spent most of his life on Santa Clara Pueblo and now lives in Mora, New Mexico. He has written several articles and one book. He teaches in the Department of Social Work at New Mexico Highlands University, fly fishes for trout, runs long distances, and seeks life daily.